THE FARM THAT FEEDS US

Nancy Castaldo

Illustrated by Ginnie Hsu

words & pictures

For my wonderful agent/friend, Jennifer Laughran, who finds joy in books, farmer's markets, and growing her own tomatoes. This one's for you!—N C

For my sweet grandmother, Zhang Yang Lai Yu, who taught me about kindness, compassion, and cooking with fresh ingredients. I love you so much—G H

Brimming with creative inspiration, how-to projects, and useful information to enrich your everyday life, quarto.com is a favorite destination for those pursuing their interests and passions.

First published in 2020 by words & pictures,
an imprint of The Quarto Group.
100 Cummings Center, Suite 265D
Beverly, MA 01915, USA.
T (978) 282-9590
F (978) 283-2742
www.quarto.com

Editor: **Emily Pither**
Consultant: **Vicki Leng, The Country Trust**
Designer: **Karen Hood**
Art Director: **Susi Martin**
Creative Director: **Malena Stojic**
Publisher: **Maxime Boucknooghe**

A CIP record for this book is available from the Library of Congress.

ISBN 978-0-7112-4253-1
eISBN 978-0-7112-5495-4

Manufactured in **Guangdong, China** TT062022

9 8 7 6 5

CONTENTS

FARMING AND FEEDING 4
TYPES OF FARM 6

SPRING 8
INSIDE THE CHICKEN COOP 10
AT THE ORCHARD 12
TILLING THE FIELDS 14
FARM MACHINERY 16
HARVESTING EARLY
    SPRING CROPS 18
OFF TO MARKET 20
SHEEP IN SPRINGTIME 22

SUMMER 24
PICK-YOUR-OWN 26
CORN PLANTING AND
    HARVESTING 28
IN THE HIVE 30
MOWING HAY 32
MILKING COWS 34
DIVERSITY IS LIFE! 36
HEADING TO THE
    COUNTY FAIR 38
FROM FARM TO TABLE 40
POLLINATING THE FARM 42
NATURAL PEST CONTROL 44
PLANTING COOL-WEATHER
    CROPS 46

FALL 48
HARVESTING PUMPKINS 50
PIES AND PRESERVES 52
PUTTING THE FIELDS TO SLEEP .. 54
FALL GRAZING 56
ANIMALS ON THE FARM 58

WINTER 60
WINTER MAINTENANCE 62
WINTER CARE OF BEES 64
TRIMMING AND PRUNING
    THE ORCHARD 66
SEED SHOPPING 68
BAKING BREAD 70
AT THE FARMER'S MARKET 72
CARING FOR EQUIPMENT 74
FEEDING THE ANIMALS 76

DOING OUR BIT 78
GLOSSARY 80

FARMING AND FEEDING

Hurray for farms that supply us with the food we eat!
Some farmers grow crops like corn, tomatoes, and wheat.
Some farmers raise animals, like pigs,
chickens, and cows. Some do both.

Farming has changed over the years. In the past, farmers
used to run small farms with enough animals and crops
to feed their family. Today, there are more large farms
owned by corporations, which often farm in just one
type of crop or animal. But small family farms still
exist and many are helping to keep our planet,
and the species that live here, healthy and
thriving for many years to come.

Some farmers bring their foods to markets to sell and share with their communities. They sometimes grow and raise heritage and heirloom breeds, which look and taste like they have done for hundreds of years. These farmers help to keep our food varied and yummy.

Farmers, whether they grow vegetables or provide us with the milk we drink or the meat we eat, keep us healthy and strong.

Let's take a look at a farm that feeds us all year round.

TYPES OF FARM

There are many kinds of farms. Big and small.
On all farms, the days are filled with busy work.
Every season brings new life, new chores,
and food for us to eat.

Dairy farms

Dairy farms keep lots of
animals, like cows and
goats, that give us milk.
These farms produce
milk, cheese, and butter.

Poultry farms

Poultry farms raise chickens,
turkeys, and other birds for
food and eggs.

Industrial vs free-range

Many farms raise animals, called livestock, for us to eat,
but not all farms treat their livestock the same way.
Industrial farms are big and often treat their animals
with medicines and chemicals to keep them healthy and
make them grow large. The animals may be kept in
cramped quarters and are not able to practice their
natural behaviors. Free-range farms are thought to be
more ethical because animals are allowed to move
about more freely. Animals are treated more
kindly and are able to behave naturally.

Arable farms

On arable farms, the land is not used for grazing animals. Instead, the earth is plowed, either by tractor or by animal power. Once plowed, seeds are planted so that crops can grow.

Sheep farms

Sheep farms raise sheep for food and also for wool and milk. Certain cheeses, like pecorino and feta, are made from sheep's milk.

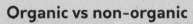

Orchards

Farms with rows and rows of trees that give us fruit and nuts are called orchards. They might grow apples, peaches, or almonds.

Organic vs non-organic
Non-organic farms use man-made fertilizers and chemicals on their crops to improve the soil and to control pests and weeds. Chemicals that kill pests, like beetles and weevils, are called pesticides. These can be harmful to animals, humans, and the environment. Farms that practice more natural farming methods and use less pest and weed killing chemicals are thought to be safer for our planet.

SPRING

It's spring on the farm! The days grow longer, and birds begin to sing early in the morning. But the farmer is awake even before the birds start chirping. Animals need to be fed. Cows and goats need to be milked.

Barn

Cow milking shed

Farmhouse

Chicken coop

Pick-your-own fields

Orchard

Bee hives

Fields

INSIDE THE CHICKEN COOP

A coop is a small house where the chickens live to keep them safe. The rooster guards the hens—*Cock a doodle doo* it bellows when anyone comes near, even the farmer. Can you see any eggs in the coop?

What do chickens eat?

Chickens eat insects and seeds in the wild. On many industrial farms, chickens are kept in cages and are fed by machines, but on this farm, the chickens are free range which means that they can feed themselves as they roam about. Since these chickens are in the coop, the farmer adds some grain. *Peck, peck, peck.*

Laying eggs

Chickens lay lots of eggs in spring. Some types of hen lay speckled eggs, some lay long, narrow eggs, while others lay rounder eggs. If there aren't too many hens, the farmer can tell which has laid each egg by its shape and color. Hurray, each hen in the coop has laid an egg and they are gathered up. The farmer counts: *five, six, seven...* Soon there will be dozens! Some will be served for breakfast and the rest will go to market.

Chicken breeds

There are many breeds of chickens in this coop. Some are brown, some are speckled, and some are black and white. Having a variety of different chickens on the farm lets the farmer have eggs all year. Old, heritage breeds are not as common on a farm, but make a flock more diverse.

Hamburg
Lays about 200 glossy white eggs per year.

Rhode Island Red
Lays about 250 eggs per year.

Ameraucana
Lays about 250 beautiful blue-green eggs per year.

Brahma
Lays around 150 eggs per year.

Leghorn
Lays around 280-300 eggs per year.

Plymouth Rock
Lays around 200 eggs per year.

Egg hatching

The month of March is chick hatching time. Some chickens are "broody," meaning that they sit on their eggs until they hatch. Eggs must be fertilized to become chicks.

AT THE ORCHARD

During the spring months, the orchard comes to life. Beautiful blossoms arrive, filling the apple tree branches with soft pink and white flowers. The trees will grow quickly as they have lots of energy in the spring from sugars stored in their roots.

Orchard fruits

These are common fruits that grow in orchards. Most fruits appear during the summer months.

Apples

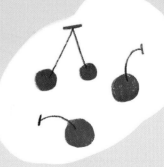

Cherries

Checking the bee hives

As soon as the days grow warmer, it is time for the farmer to check the honey bees in the hives. Peeking in, the farmer can see all shades of pollen, from pale yellow to bright orange, from all the early spring flowers. The bees have been busy. They use pollen for food, but as they gather it, they also pollinate the plants, helping them to grow, breed, and produce food. This important process is key to maintaining a healthy environment, as well as providing habitats for other creatures.

Thanks to the bees, soon there will be all kinds of fruits and vegetables on the farm. But not everything has been planted yet... First the farmer must prepare the soil.

Pears

Plums

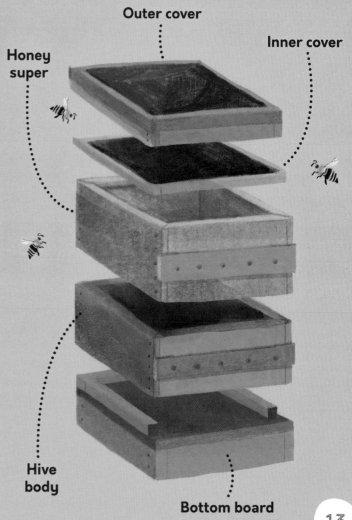

Outer cover

Inner cover

Honey super

Hive body

Bottom board

13

TILLING THE FIELDS

Out comes the tractor pulling a plow behind it. The farmer climbs into the cab, starts the engine, and drives the tractor into the field. The plow cuts through the soil and makes small ditches called furrows. Then it's time to sow the seeds into them.

What will grow?

This spring, the farmer plants a variety of fresh vegetables.

Lettuce

Carrots

Beans

Radishes

Beets

Peas

FARM MACHINERY

Farmers use many kinds of equipment and machinery. Some are used by hand and others are big enough to ride and drive.

Tractor

Tractors might be the most important piece of equipment on the farm. They can plow, plant, pull grain carts, and even move snow. Most tractors have two small wheels and two large wheels. Some tractors have tracks, like an armored tank, that help move the machine along.

Manure spreader

A manure, or muck, spreader is used to distribute manure over a field as a fertilizer. It is usually attached to the back of a tractor and is pulled through the field.

Livestock trailer

Livestock trailers help the farmer move animals from place to place.

Combine harvester

Combines have a different job. They help the farmer harvest crops, like corn.

Baler

A baler is a machine used for turning cut hay into neat bales that are easy to handle, transport, and store.

Bale wrapper

The farmer uses a bale wrapper to cover the hay with plastic to protect it. The bales are often left outside in the field once wrapped.

Bale lifter

The bale lifter picks up the heavy bales. The bales are heavy, so the farmer needs a lifter to help move them.

Hand tools

Hay fork
A hay fork is a tool with a long handle and two or more sharp metal prongs, used for lifting hay or straw.

Shovel
A shovel is a long-handled tool with a wide blade, used for digging, lifting, and moving materials such as soil.

Sickle
A sickle is a short-handled tool with a semicircular blade, used for harvesting, or cutting, crops.

HARVESTING EARLY SPRING CROPS

Fresh, leafy vegetables sprout in cool soil, so they are perfect for early spring planting. Soon, it's time for picking.

Peas

Peas are planted after the snow melts. Soon shoots peek up. Garden peas, snow peas, and snap peas. Pick them young for the sweetest flavor.

Lettuces and greens

The outer leaves of lettuce plants are plucked by hand. There are so many different kinds of lettuces and greens to make a yummy spring salad. Green leaf. Red leaf. Spiky mizuna. Crunchy spinach. Perfectly picked from the spring garden.

Asparagus

This tasty vegetable is planted once and enjoyed for years to come. The pencil-sized spears poke through the soil in spring and are cut or plucked from the base to bring to table.

Radishes

Radish leaves sprout above the ground while crunchy radish roots grow big below, ready to be sliced for a spring salad. Radishes come in all sizes and colors.

OFF TO MARKET

Everyone is eager for fresh food from the farm in the spring. For many farms, it's the first chance to have fresh, local greens after a long winter. Farm markets help farmers sell their produce and products they have made, like tangy cheese or sweet, sweet honey. Markets can also be a wonderful place to meet neighbors and enjoy tasty, fresh food. Buying locally helps everyone. It reduces transportation, which is better for the planet and provides us with healthy food choices.

The farm gets busy. Eggs are gathered. Blue, white, and brown. Lettuce is picked. Leafy green, red, and spiky. Crunchy radishes are washed. Red, white, and pink.

The farmer packs up the truck. Time to head to market.

SHEEP IN SPRINGTIME

The weather is getting warmer. Days are getting longer.
Lambs are born. There are many breeds of sheep.
Some are raised for meat and some for their wool.

Lambing

Green hills are perfect grazing land for sheep, so their feet do not get soggy in damp valleys. In the early spring, new lambs are born to female sheep, which are called ewes. The new little lambs drink milk from their mother and stay close by her side.

Shearing

The sheep are fluffy and warm. As the weather gets hotter in late spring or early summer, it is time for the sheep to be sheared to keep them cool. The shorn sheep prance around the fields. Like a haircut, the soft wool falls to the ground. Brown, white, and cream. The wool will be used for sweaters and socks. A natural fiber, wool is better for our planet than clothes made from petroleum-based acrylic or chemically made polyester.

Sheep breeds

Merino

Merino sheep produce much loved fine wool. They are one of the oldest breeds of sheep in the world.

Icelandic

These sheep live in harsher climates and on mountains. They produce coarser wool that is often used in rugs and heavy sweaters. Their wool comes in a variety of colors.

Cotswold

This English breed has a fleece that grows long and produces fibers that feel silky. The Cotswold is a "threatened" breed because there are not many left.

Lincoln

The Lincoln, which comes from England, is one of the world's largest breeds of sheep. It is said to have the heaviest and thickest fleece of any breed. Unfortunately, it is also listed as "threatened."

Corriedale

Corriedale sheep are the grandchildren and great grandchildren of lambs that had one Merino parent and one Lincoln parent. The Corriedale is the most common sheep in New Zealand, where sheep outnumber people ten to one!

Dorset

Dorset ewes can have lambs all year round, making them a popular sheep on farms around the world. They are kept for both meat and milk.

SUMMER

It's summer! Spring rains and winds have brought down the apple blossoms, but now the tree branches are cloaked with green leaves. Those leaves turn sunlight into food through photosynthesis. Some of that food will keep the tree growing but some will be stored in the roots to help the tree survive the coming cold months.

If you look closely, you can see tiny apples forming where the flowers once were. The farmer looks carefully at each branch, then plucks off some of the little apples so that the tree's energy can go into growing fewer, bigger apples.

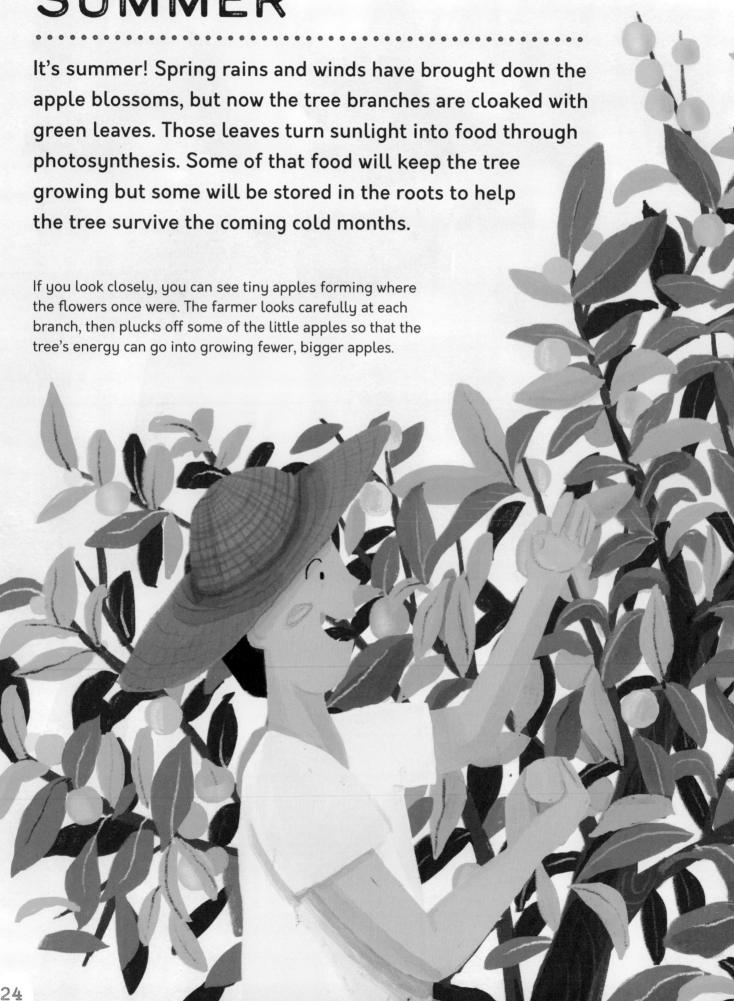

Photosynthesis

Let's take a closer look at what happens during photosynthesis.

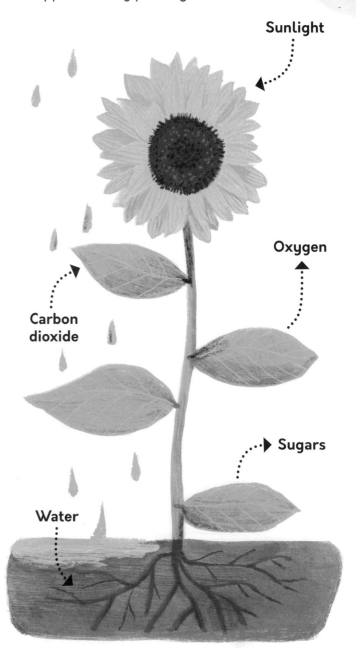

Sunlight

Oxygen

Carbon dioxide

Sugars

Water

Plants take in a gas called carbon dioxide through their leaves, while they soak up water from the soil through their roots. Using sunlight as their fuel, plants turn these ingredients into sugars, which they use as food. Photosynthesis also produces oxygen, which plants release into the air. Although plants don't need that oxygen, it is very useful for us, as we need to breathe oxygen to survive.

PICK-YOUR-OWN

Rows and rows of green leaves hide juicy, red strawberries underneath. It's time for visitors to come to the farm for pick-your-own season. No sprays to kill weeds or pests are used on the thin-skinned fruit, so they are ready to be picked and popped into a waiting mouth—no washing needed. Rhubarb bunches are offered at the farm stand for visitors to make delicious rhubarb pies.

Strawberries ·····

Raspberries ·········

Cherries

Rhubarb

CORN PLANTING AND HARVESTING

Corn first grew wild in the Americas. Today, farmers plant corn for people to eat or for livestock to eat. Some large farms also grow corn that will be turned into fuel.

Planting

Out comes the plow. It's two weeks since the last frost, so it's time to plant the corn. Corn is also called maize. Vroom vroom. The farmer drives across the field.

Rows and rows of corn kernels, which are the plant's seeds, are planted.

There are many types of corn: sweet, field, and popcorn are just a few. And soon green shoots appear.

Harvesting

The first ears of corn will be ready to harvest in about two months. Each stalk will give the farmer several ears, while each ear gives around 800 kernels. Corn is sweetest on the day it is picked. Most sweet corn are yellow, white, or two-colored. Other varieties of corn, which are used for cornmeal and popcorn, come in many different colors, like blue, purple, and red. Cornmeal can be made into delicious tortillas and tamales. Some varieties of corn have ears filled with kernels that look like multi-colored gems.

Heirloom corn varieties

Glass gem
This colorful variety is one of the most beautiful. It was bred by Cherokee corn collector Carl "White Eagle" Barnes.

Bloody butcher dent corn
This solid red corn is ground for flour.

Buhl sweet corn
This delicious yellow sweet corn is a favorite at summer picnics.

IN THE HIVE

The worker honey bees have been busy visiting all the flowers on the farm, collecting pollen that they turn into honey. Now it is time to gather the rich golden honey they have made. Tasty honey is stirred into tea and spread on golden toast.

Honey tastes

Honeys have different tastes, depending on where the bees collected the nectar. Wildflower honey is created from a variety of field flower nectar. Buckwheat, on the other hand, has a stronger taste and is made from the nectar of buckwheat flowers.

Honey collecting

The beekeeper wears a special hat with a net to protect them from stings. Beekeepers use a machine called a bee smoker. Smoke from burning pine needles keeps the bees calm during collection. Different sections of the hive, called screens, are lifted out of the box. Bees are shaken off the honeycomb, which is made of beeswax shaped into hexagonal cells. Clever bees make beeswax, too. The honeycomb is where bees store their honey and eggs. The wax is scraped, releasing the honey.

Honey is a tasty treat given to us by bees but bees are also very important because the majority of plants we need for food rely on pollination. Bees are key to the varied, colorful, and nutritious diets we need and enjoy.

Bee products

Raw honey still contains pollen carried by bees from the blooms they visited. Many people prefer raw honey because it has added nutrients from the pollen. Most honey sold in stores is filtered, so it does not contain any pollen. Then it is heated at high temperatures, leaving it clean, smooth, and clear. Beeswax can be eaten or used for candles and sweet-smelling salve to heal and smoothe rough hands.

MOWING HAY

Let's make hay! Dried grass, alfalfa, and other green plants make a tasty, healthy diet for cows, sheep, and horses. To make hay, the farmer must mow and rake the grass three times during the growing season. The Sun's warmth dries the grass into hay before it is baled, or wrapped into large bundles. Hay bales can be round or square.

MILKING COWS

Cows produce milk to feed their calves. They can also produce milk for us to drink after their calf is born. The milk can be used to make cheese, yogurt, and other dairy foods we eat. Cows need to be milked twice a day, by hand or machine.

Milking machines

On some industrial farms, cows are kept in pens and are bred to produce unnaturally high volumes of milk. On this organic, family farm, the cows are free to roam around fields that are free from pesticides. Cows on the organic farm receive little or no antibiotics or hormones to increase milk production. This makes milk healthier for people to drink.

Teat cups

Tank

Milk tube

Breeds

There are many different dairy cows, but all breeds provide milk. Here are a few common breeds.

Holstein
Holsteins are large cattle with black and white patches on their bodies. An individual Holstein cow can produce over 72,000 pounds of milk in a year.

Jersey
With their fawn coat, Jersey cows are one of the most recognized and well-known breeds. Jerseys are small but they produce rich and creamy milk.

Guernsey
Like Jerseys, this breed also came from the Channel Islands between England and France. They have light brown spots. Guernsey milk contains more calcium, vitamins, and protein than average milk.

Brown Swiss
Considered the oldest breed, Brown Swiss cattle come from the Alpine pastures of Switzerland. Their milk is excellent for cheese production.

Ayrshire
Ayrshires come from Scotland and have reddish brown spots on their white bodies. Milk from Ayrshires is great for making ice cream.

DIVERSITY IS LIFE!

Many say that variety is the spice of life. There is no better place to experience the goodness of variety than on a small farm, where the farmer grows a choice of delicious fruits and vegetables. Every different plant offers us different tastes and nutrition. Each time a farmer saves seeds and plants a heritage or heirloom fruit or vegetable, we get even more choice and goodness.

Supporting farmers

Buying produce from small farms allows us to know if farming practices are sustainable and ethical. You can help farmers by shopping at farmers' markets or buying a share in community supported agriculture (CSA). The money the shareholders pay to the farmer at the beginning of the year helps with the upkeep of the farm. In return, the shareholders get a weekly assortment of ripe produce, and sometimes flowers, through the growing season.

Diversity helps our food security. If one species suffers from a disease or insect invasion, another species might survive to feed us.

This week's share includes a bouquet of sunflowers, tomatoes, green peppers, and some heirloom red noodle beans to try. A new recipe is tucked into the bag!

HEADING TO THE COUNTY FAIR

It's time for the county fair! A favorite time of the year. A time of amusement rides, games, and contests. Everybody on the farm gets ready. Farmers come from all over the county to show off their produce and livestock.

Ducks, roosters, and rabbits sit on display. Lots of breeds to see.

Cows are washed and groomed. Ribbons are handed out for the best in each breed.

The sheep are shorn. The soft wool is spun for display.

Horses parade around the track, showing off their shiny coats and braided manes.

The tractors chug, chug, chug with lots of weight during the tractor pull.

Who will have the most perfect peppers this year?

Beans win ribbons for shape and uniformity of color.

POPCORN

Cotton candy, baked potatoes, and fried dough are sold to hungry visitors.

FIRST PRIZE

Blueberries are picked and washed. Grandma's blueberry pie wins the pie contest.

The first-place basil is deep green. Even the most unusual vegetable gets a prize.

FROM FARM TO TABLE

The spring chicks are now beginning to lay eggs. The fresh eggs are tasty for breakfast and even tastier when they are used to make a loaf of tasty zucchini bread.

It's a special day. A chef from a local restaurant is visiting the farm. Restaurant chefs are eager to add the fresh produce and heirloom varieties to their menus. The farmer is eager to hear what the chef is planning to cook and can't wait to let the chef taste the latest crops. Squash blossoms, tomatoes, and radishes are picked and packed for the chef to take back to the kitchen for tonight's menu.

Food distribution

After crops are grown and livestock is raised, farmers deliver their goods to markets or to places where the food will be manufactured. It is made into a range of products before being distributed to supermarkets. Shoppers and chefs make their selections. Food is cooked and served on tables around the world. Our food production system allows us to feed the billions of people on our planet a variety of amazing types of food. However, the distances food travels can contribute to pollution and have a negative impact on the environment. Buying locally grown and produced food helps with this. It also helps us to understand where our food comes from and where it goes. Here's how food distribution works, from farm to your table:

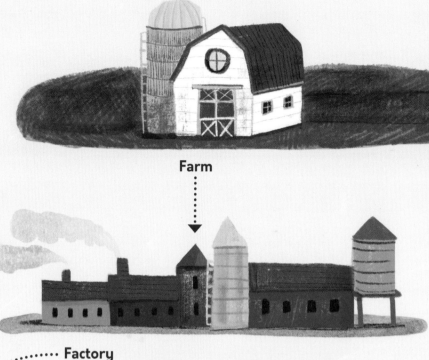

Farm

Factory

Distribution

Supermarket

Restaurant

Home

POLLINATING THE FARM

The summer garden is planted with all sorts of flowers. With their sweet nectar, flowers attract bees, butterflies, birds, and other wildlife that pollinate the plants. Without pollinators transporting flower pollen from flower to flower, many of the plants on the farm could not produce fruits and vegetables. Farmers plant wildflowers and allow grasses to flower instead of mowing them. Areas of unmanaged wild woodland and hedges, free from harmful pesticides, also keep pollinators happy and busy.

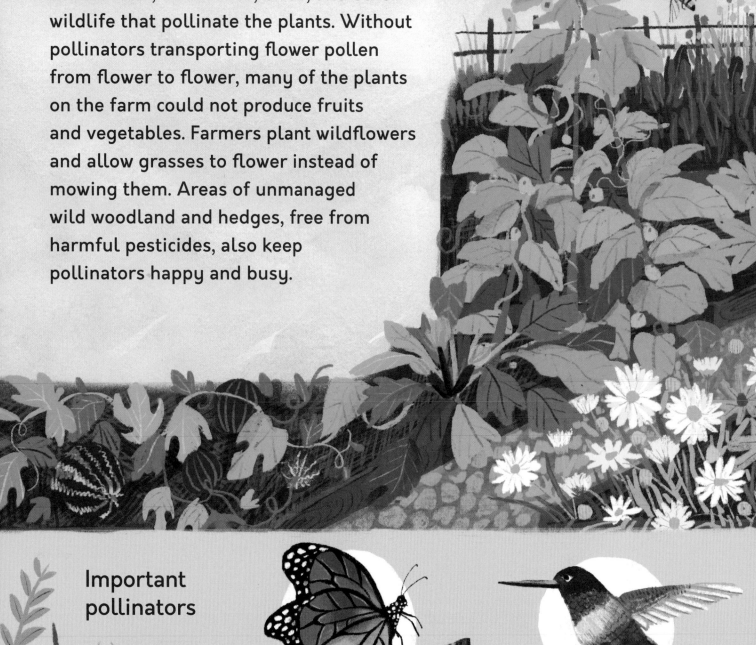

Mosquitoes

Important pollinators

Butterflies and moths
These winged insects also help pollinate plants on the farm.

Hummingbirds
Hummingbirds flit, with fast wings, from flower to flower, lapping up their nectar with their long tongue. Hummers pick up pollen as they visit each plant.

Beetles

Wasps

Ants

Honey bees
These bees pollinate apple trees, broccoli, almonds, melons, cranberries, cherries, and other crops.

Bumblebees
Bumblebees pollinate field beans, strawberries, tomatoes, eggplants, peppers, and many other crops.

Hoverflies
Hoverflies, also called flower flies, not only pollinate many fruit crops, but also prey on other insects that harm plants.

NATURAL PEST CONTROL

Some insects and other creepy-crawlies are a pest because they nibble on crops. Large farms often use manmade pesticides to keep pests under control, but some farms use natural pest control, which can be less harmful to the environment. Organic farms use many different methods, including crop rotation, crop isolation, and growing other plants nearby that ward off pests. Farmers also encourage other insects, like ladybugs and midge flies, that prey on harmful pests.

Rotating crops

Changing the crops year to year is called crop rotation. It keeps the farm healthy, because different pests are attracted by different crops, so no particular pest will get out of control. Last year the farmer planted soybeans in the field. Planting corn in the field this year will keep the soil healthy, as different crops also use up different nutrients in the soil. If crops are regularly changing, weeds also do not have a chance to adapt to the situation, so farmers also need to use less chemical weedkiller.

Isolating crops

Growing crops away from each other, with lots of space around them, means pests have more trouble traveling between them. If farmers have plenty of room, they can also move crops from place to place, year by year, so sweet potato weevils will have difficulty following the sweet potatoes. The simplest method of isolating crops is to use row covers. Farmers protect their crops by covering them with a layer of material to prevent pesky insects from getting inside.

Warding off pests

Some plants have a strong smell that keeps pests away. The lovely scent of lavender isn't liked by moths, fleas, and flies. Peppermint is not the favorite stench of aphids, cabbage beetles, and squash bugs. Colorful marigolds look harmless but repel lots of insects.

PLANTING COOL-WEATHER CROPS

Planting time again! Even though it is still summer, some crops that grow better in the cooler, fall season need to be planted now. Some will be harvested during the fall and some will need to grow over winter.

Crops for late summer planting

Garlic
Garlic is planted in late summer and early fall. It won't be harvested until the following summer.

Spinach
Spinach can be planted in late summer and harvested during the coming cool months.

Peas
Planting peas in the heat of summer will give the farmer a fall crop.

Beets
Plant beets from June until
September to harvest in the fall.
Leaves and roots can be eaten.

Collards
Plant mid- to late summer
to harvest in the fall.

Turnips
Sow turnips in late summer to
enjoy a harvest before winter.

FALL

Fall has arrived. The days are getting cooler and shorter. The leaves are beginning to turn shades of yellow, brown, and scarlet. But the growing season hasn't ended yet. The orchard is filled with shiny green and red apples. There are many different apple varieties. Some are great for cooking, some for eating, and some for both! Pick, pick, pick. Crunch, crunch, crunch.

Types of apple

Here are a few favorite apple varieties.

Baldwin

Some apple varieties are very old, like the shiny, red Baldwin from the 1700s. The Baldwin was sometimes called "Woodpecker" because trees are often visited by woodpeckers.

Calville Blanc d'Hiver

French curvy, lobed green Calville Blanc d'Hiver dates from 1598. It was grown on President Thomas Jefferson's Virginia estate, Monticello.

Honeycrisp

The light yellow and red Honeycrisp is a new hybrid, developed in Minnesota in 1974. It came on the market in 1991 and is one of the post popular apples in America.

Macoun

Ruby red with streaks of yellow-green, the Macoun has a crisp white juicy center, perfect for eating.

HARVESTING PUMPKINS

Every day, the pumpkins grow bigger and bigger in the field. Round and oval. Tall and small. Orange, white, and pink. Smooth and knobby. So many choices for Halloween and baking. Farmers cut the squash off the vines with sharp pruners. Pumpkins are often left in the fields for pick-your-own fall fun.

Pumpkin varieties

Here are some perfect pumpkins for eating and showing this fall.

Galeux d'Eysines
A flattened, round pumpkin with peachy-pink skin and large warts. This French heirloom is delicious in soups.

New England sugar pie
This small, round orange pumpkin is perfect for pies.

Kogigu
This bumpy, ribbed pumpkin will never turn orange. It will remain a deep green. The kogigu originated in Japan.

Fortna white pumpkin
This pear-shaped white pumpkin looks like a Halloween ghost in the making.

Jack be little
A teeny tiny orange pumpkin that is perfect for a tabletop.

PIES AND PRESERVES

Back in the farmhouse kitchen, it's time to turn the farm's freshly picked fruit and vegetables into something delicious. Mouths water from the smells of sweet cinnamon and tangy vinegar filling the air.

Jams

Bowls of plump raspberries are emptied into pots on the stove. *Simmer, simmer.* Sweet jam will be spread on warm bread this winter.

Pies

Chop, chop, chop. Apples are sliced and put in waiting pie dough. Brown sugar, cinnamon, oats, and butter are mixed together to make a crumbly topping.

Sauces

Snip, snip, snip. Basil leaves are cut, rinsed, and dried. Chopped nuts are added, olive oil is drizzled, and everything is blended together into a paste. Pungent pesto for pasta will be frozen, ready to use during the rest of the year.

Chutneys

Tart apples are boiled with sugar, onions, ginger, vinegar, and spices until the mixture turns dark, jammy, and shiny. Spicy apple chutney will be poured into jars, ready to be sealed and brought to market.

PUTTING THE FIELDS TO SLEEP

The entire farm gets ready for the cold ahead. After all the crops have been harvested, the farmer still needs to tend to the fields and the orchards. The fields need to be put to sleep to keep the soil healthy for the spring plantings. Healthy soil will feed the growing seeds. Every part of the farm needs to be ready for winter.

Planting cover crops

Planting a cover crop in the fall, after the harvest, helps the farm keep important nutrients, like nitrogen, in the soil for the next crop. The roots hold fast in the dirt and will keep it in place when winter storms batter the land. The farmer will pick a cover crop that will be the most helpful to the future crop.

Mowing the orchard

When leaves fall, the farmer needs to mow the orchard to speed up leaf decomposition. As leaves decompose, they release lots of nutrients back into the soil. The chopped up, mown leaves will serve as a compost around the trees during the winter.

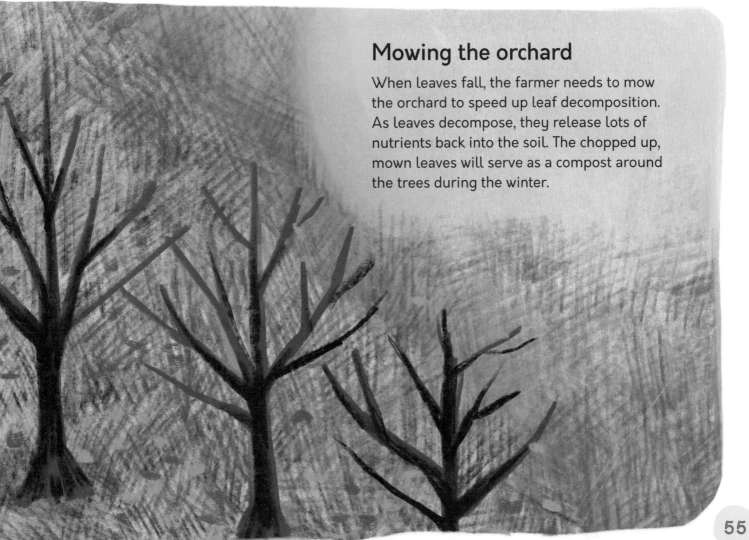

FALL GRAZING

All the different livestock help the farm in different ways. Chickens eat weeds and problem bugs, while giving the farmer eggs. Goats clear brush and provide milk. Pigs eat everything, like weeds and garden waste. They also give the farmer important manure to help fertilize the crops.

Free-ranging pigs

Fall gives pigs an opportunity to roll around in the mud and eat foods of the forest. Think of the saying, "pig out." On some farms, pigs are free-ranging, so they can forage for natural, woodland food like hickory nuts, mushrooms, grubs, roots, and acorns. Pigs that are woodland-foraging are healthier and become healthier meat for people who enjoy bacon, chops, and other pork. They also seem to be happier.

Pig breeds

Let's take a closer look at some common pig breeds.

Tamworth

This breed originated in England, is on the smaller side, and is considered a "threatened" breed. Tamworth pigs are red in color.

Chester White

These popular pigs are great mothers. They are all white, sometimes with small spots.

Large Black

These pigs enjoy foraging for food. They have floppy ears.

Hampshire

The Hampshire was imported from Britain. A Hampshire pig has a black body with a white band circling the front legs and back.

Gloucestershire Old Spot

This threatened pig species from England has lop ears and is considered an orchard pig.

Ossabaw Island

The Ossabaw comes from the United States via the Canary Islands. It's highly sociable, so perfect for farms with many animals.

ANIMALS ON THE FARM

There are many animals on the farm besides the pigs, chickens, sheep, and cows. Here are some of the others that might live on the farm. Some of them help the farmer with their work. Others spend lots of time relaxing in the sunshine.

Horses

Horses munch in the pasture or eat hay in the barn. They can be used for riding.

Alpacas

Alpacas grow soft wool. They don't require much land and are fun for farmers to raise. They are protective animals and can also be used to help guard sheep.

Ducks

There are many breeds of ducks that make happy additions to a family farm. They roam free and provide eggs to the farmer.

Cats

Barn cats lie in the sunshine and keep mice and rats out of the hay in the barn.

Dogs

Many dogs help with work on the farm. They might herd sheep or help round up ducks in the evening.

Goats

Goats are raised for their meat and their milk. They also do a great job of eating weeds.

WINTER

Soft snow falls on the farm and all seems quiet. The growing season has ended, but the farm is still busy. There is lots to do during the winter, inside and outdoors, so that the farm is ready for the next year. It is time for the farmer to catch up on repairs and plan for spring planting.

WINTER MAINTENANCE

As the weather gets colder, it's time for the farmer to prepare the farm for the chilly winter months ahead. The farmer gets out brooms for sweeping, hoses for cleaning, and hammers and nails for fixing, mending, and building.

Repairing the barn

Old birds' nests are removed and cobwebs and dust are cleaned away. This gets the barn ready for any livestock that will spend the winter inside. Branches that might break under the weight of heavy ice and snow are pruned, and the barn roof is inspected to prevent winter leaks. Hinges are greased. Holes are filled. Sorry, mice!

Cleaning out the chicken coop

Winter means roosting time inside the coop. The hens need air to flow in and out during the cold months, but not too much. A drafty coop will make it damp and cold. The chickens will stay warm and dry when new straw and kiln dried wood shavings are added. Since the hens will be inside more than outside in winter, the coop will need more regular cleaning to keep it warm and dry.

Splitting wood

Firewood makes the home smell sweet as it warms. Old farmhouse or new farmhouse, a wood stove makes winter warmer, keeping the farmer's family nice and cozy. Wood trimmed from the orchard and other farm trees is split by the farmer with a sharp axe to fit nicely in the stove during the cold months.

WINTER CARE OF BEES

Bees are very important to the farm's crops, so the farmer is worried that the number of bees around the world is falling. No one is quite sure why, but it probably has something to do with pesticides and climate change. All bees are important, both wild bumblebees and the farmer's hives of honey bees. The farmer must take extra care to ready them all for the cold months ahead and their emergence in the spring.

Keeping honey bees warm

The honey bee hives are wrapped in black tar paper to keep them dry and warm in the winter. The farmer has already made sure that the hives will spend the cold months in a sunny spot. The top lid of the hive is tilted just a little to let air in for the wintering bees. Since there is no food for the bees outside, the farmer has added a block of sugar fondant to the hive for them to eat during the winter.

Helping native bees in the orchard

Some hay bales are left in the orchard after mowing. Sleepy field mice nest in them over winter, but after the mice leave in spring, bumblebees use the holes in the hay for nesting. Those bumbles will join the honey bees to become perfect pollinators for the orchard in the spring.

TRIMMING AND PRUNING THE ORCHARD

The apple trees are dormant all winter, which means they are not growing, just resting. In a few months, when spring arrives, flowers will bloom from the branches. Pruning and trimming the trees when they are naked of leaves, flowers, and fruit lets the farmer see the tree better to be able to shape it to keep it healthy. Pruning now means there will be lots of apples to pick next fall.

SEED SHOPPING

Snow may be falling, but spring is just around the corner. Seed shopping makes the winter go by faster. The farmer selects some heirloom seeds to try in the coming growing season. It's fun to experiment with a new crop. Perhaps a new heritage lettuce, heirloom pepper, or purple carrots? So many choices.

Heirloom seeds

Some heirloom seeds have been saved for many generations. Each variety tells a story of where they began and how they were saved. Older varieties provide special tastes, colors, shapes, and nutrition. They also make favorite meals exciting and new. Let's take a closer look at a few different varieties.

Brandywine Tomato

One of the most popular heirloom varieties, this large dark tomato was first grown in 1885.

Missouri Heirloom Yellow-Flesh Watermelon

This is an old variety that has sweet, yellow-orange flesh.

Fish Peppers

An African-American heirloom, this pepper has its roots in the mid-Atlantic region of the United States. It has a great Caribbean flavor.

Roman artichoke

This medium artichoke comes from the Puglia region in Italy, the site of an annual artichoke festival.

Purple-Podded Dutch Bean

Believed to have been grown by Capuchin monks in the 16th century, these peas with purple pods are a favorite Dutch variety.

Kidd's orange red apple

This is a cross between two old varieties: Cox's Orange Pippen and Red Delicious. It originated in 1924.

69

BAKING BREAD

Flour, yeast, salt, and water are used to make fresh bread in the kitchen. Mix, knead, pound, bake. The oven warms the room and soon the smell of baking bread fills the farm kitchen. Loaves to eat with the farmer's meals and loaves to sell at the farmer's market.

Make your own bread

Ingredients
3 cups flour
¼ tsp yeast
1 tbsp salt
1½ cups water

Method

1. In a mixing bowl, combine the flour, yeast, and salt, then add the water.

2. Cover the bowl with a tea towel. Let the dough sit while it rises for 12–18 hours.

3. Flour the surface of your counter. Tip the dough onto the floured surface. Sprinkle the dough with a little more flour and fold over a couple of times. Cover with a tea towel and let sit for 15 minutes.

4. Place your dough onto a floured towel. Cover the floured dough with another towel and let sit for 2 hours.

5. Preheat the oven to 450°F (230°C), then warm a lidded pot for 15 minutes.

6. Place the dough inside the pot and cook in the oven for 30 minutes.

7. Using gloves, take the lid off, then let the bread continue cooking in the oven. Remove when the bread is lightly browned.

8. Using oven gloves, place the bread on a cooling rack.

AT THE FARMER'S MARKET

Farmers bring their crops, bread, jam, and meats to the local farmer's market. Tables and tents are set up in lines. Fresh eggs, heirloom vegetables, cheese, and flowers are on display. Markets provide a place for farmers to sell to the public without having to provide large quantities to big supermarkets. Local markets help farmers and the environment by cutting down on the cost of transportation and the fuel used to carry food great distances. Customers come to pick up tasty, fresh foods to take home for their dinner.

CARING FOR EQUIPMENT

It's time to make sure the farm equipment is in good working order for the coming season. Oil is changed in all the engines so they will run smoothly. Filters are cleaned or replaced so machinery will stay clean. Tires are inflated. Antifreeze fluid is checked so the tractor will keep running when the temperature drops. Seeds, grain, and field greens are removed from seeders, tillers, and balers. The snow plow is readied. All equipment that won't be used during the harshest weeks is stored inside to protect them from the winter weather.

FEEDING THE ANIMALS

Even when the wind makes your nose cold, the farm animals need to be fed. The farmer rises early, bundles up, and heads to the barns. Everyone is hungry. Pigs, cows, horses, chickens, and sheep. Once she has fed the animals, it is time for the farmer to eat: breakfast is waiting inside the warm kitchen.

Winter means that the livestock are unable to graze outside for their food. Grains and feed are brought inside and stored so they are dry and away from pests.

Chicken feed is used for feeding poultry. Oatmeal is a warm food for chickens on cold winter mornings.

Hay is made of grasses and alfalfa that has been mowed, dried, and made into bales. It is served up to cows and horses during the months that they cannot go outside to graze. Field corn, oats, and barley are also fed to cows during the winter.

All livestock need fresh, clean water. During winter, some farmers use heated bowls and troughs, while some add small rubber balls that help prevent the water from freezing solid.

DOING OUR BIT

Farmers help us to stay healthy. Local farmers care for animals and the planet, provide food that helps us live well, and give us a choice of tasty products all year round, whatever the weather. We can all do our bit to support farmers who grow our carrots and raise the cows that put the milk in our oatmeal.

Ways to shop and eat

Here are some ways to support your local farms, eat sustainably, and protect our planet:

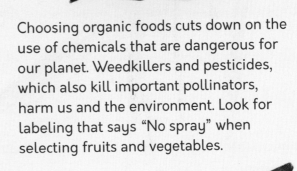

Shopping at farmers' markets not only supports local farmers but reduces the fuel used by transporting foods great distances. It is a great way to use less energy and help our planet from getting warmer.

Choosing organic foods cuts down on the use of chemicals that are dangerous for our planet. Weedkillers and pesticides, which also kill important pollinators, harm us and the environment. Look for labeling that says "No spray" when selecting fruits and vegetables.

Trying heirloom varieties protects our biodiversity, which is the total range of plants and animals living on our planet. Keeping heritage breeds and varieties alive also helps with our food security, by making sure we are not relying on a limited number of crops.

Buying only fruit and vegetables that are ripe locally reduces the distance that food has to travel. Buying food that has flown from the other side of the world uses more energy. But don't forget to support faraway farmers by shopping for fair trade choices of chocolate and coffee.

Some supermarkets are starting to sell "wonky" fruit and veggies, which is misshapen produce that would otherwise go to waste. If you see it for sale, give it a try—it's just the same, just not perfectly uniform in color, shape, and size.

Don't waste food! Remember that "Use by" dates mean that food may not be safe after the given date. But "Best before" dates just mean the food may be less good quality after that date, so check with an adult whether products are still safe to eat.

GLOSSARY

Agriculture
The practice of farming, including the growing of crops and the raising of livestock to provide food, fiber, and other products.

Antibiotics
A medicine that stops the growth of microorganisms.

Arable
Land suitable for growing crops.

Beeswax
A substance created by bees to make honeycombs.

Biodiversity
The variety of life in the world or specific habitats.

Breed
Specific animals or plants within a species having a distinct appearance and similar traits.

Carbon dioxide
A colorless, odorless gas found in our atmosphere. It is produced by animals and people breathing out, plants through photosynthesis, and by chemical reactions.

Dairy
Foods produced from milk of mammals, such as cows, goats, and buffalo.

Diversity Having variety.

Fertilizer
A chemical or a natural substance that is added to the soil to help things grow.

Fiber
A thread made from an animal or plant that is used to create cloth.

Fleece
The woolly covering of a sheep or goat.

Food security
Having reliable access to affordable, nutritious food.

Free range
Livestock kept in natural conditions instead of pens or cages.

Heirloom
An old variety of flower, fruit, or vegetable.

Heritage
An old variety of a species of livestock.

Honey
The sticky, sweet substance made by bees from nectar.

Hormones
Substances that stimulate cells or tissues into action.

Livestock
Farm animals such as cows, horses, goats, and pigs.

Manure
Animal dung that is used to fertilize land.

Nectar
The sugary fluid produced by plants. Bees collect it and use it to make honey.

Nutrient
A substance that provides nourishment for growth.

Nutrition
Getting the food necessary for good health and growth.

Organic farming
Producing food without the use of chemical fertilizers, pesticides, or other artificial agents.

Oxygen
A colorless, odorless gas that is needed to support human and animal life.

Pest
An insect or animal that is considered harmful to crops or livestock.

Pesticide
A chemical used to kill pests.

Photosynthesis
The process by which plants use sunlight to create foods from carbon dioxide and water.

Pollen
Tiny grains created by plants for fertilization.

Pollinate
The process by which plants are fertilized and reproduce.

Poultry
The meat of a chicken or other bird.

Roosting
Settling in a group for sleep or rest.

Shareholder
An owner of part of a company.

Threatened
The classification of a species of plant or animal that is facing a decrease in population.